I0528347

Compare and Contrast

99 WRITING PROMPTS FOR COMPARISON ESSAYS

Alphabet Publishing

www.AlphabetPublish.com

Copyright Alphabet Publishing 2022

ISBN: 978-1-956159-14-1 (print)

978-1-956159-15-8 (ebook)

All rights reserved. Our authors work hard to develop original, high-quality content. Please respect their efforts and their rights under copyright law. Do not copy, photocopy, or reproduce this book or any part of this book for use inside or outside the classroom, in commercial or non-commercial settings. It is also forbidden to copy, adapt, or reuse this book or any part of this book for use on websites, blogs, or third-party lesson-sharing websites.

Cover photo by yamonstro/DepositPhotos.

For permission requests, write to the publisher "ATTN: Permissions", at the address below:

Alphabet Publishing

1204 Main Street #172

Branford, CT 06405 USA

info@alphabetpublishingbooks.com

www.alphabetpublishingbooks.com

Discounts on class sets and bulk orders available upon inquiry.

Table of Contents

How to Write

Categories of Topics

Why Write Compare and Contrast Essays?

Compare and contrast essays are common on standardized tests such as the TOEFL, TOEIC, and IATEFL, and even university admissions exams or applications. A good compare and contrast essay shows that you are able to discuss two (or more) subjects, find similarities and differences between them, and then recommend one over the other based on your reader's needs. So this is a test not only of your vocabulary and grammar, but also your ability to write to your reader, analyze two subjects, and give both facts and opinions about them.

One common complaint about academic essay types is that you rarely see them in real-life. However, compare and contrast essays are actually quite common, although they may not be quite as clearly structures as they are in the classroom. Many articles and websites compare things in order to tell you which one to buy. Book reviews may compare two books to help you decide what kind of people like which one. Movie and music reviews are often the same. Newspaper articles describe events and how they are similar or different to other events. Business proposals lay out different plans to recommend a course of action. Editorials and opinion pieces may describe how two subjects appear to be very different but actually have much in common., Or vice versa. Tourist guides or books about living abroad compare and contrast two cultures to help the reader know what to do in a new place.

Outside of essays, we compare and contrast in daily life all the time. We decide on a restaurant to go to with friends, pick what to buy from different options, and think about how to best spend our time. We may present options to someone while talking to them, or in a text message. And we also note similarities between books or movies, people we meet, and historical events. We also argue about which singer or sports star is the best by comparing stats and style!

So comparing and contrasting can help us make a choice by telling us what is the same and different about two products we want to buy, places we want to visit, or plans we want to enact. Comparing and contrasting can also help us understand something better by looking at how it is similar and different from something else. And comparing and contrasting can also be fun!

Outlining a Compare and Contrast Essay

There are a few ways to organize a compare and contrast essay. As we discussed, you may be comparing two things for a published review or a letter to a friend. In that case, your structure may be looser. However, if you are writing for a class or an exam, you likely need to adhere to a clear format. Every class and every test is different so be sure you know the exact requirements. However, there are two outlines of compare-contrast essay that are extremely common. The first discusses each subject in detail before comparing and giving a recommendation or preference.

This format works well for two subjects that may have different kinds of features and not be easy to compare point-by-point. For example, imagine you are talking about two kinds of people. One person may have a very kind-looking face and you want to mention that because it's one reason you like them. It would be awkward to say "X has a kind-looking case. By contrast, Y is not kind-looking."

With One-at-a-Time Model, you can discuss the important points of each subject without feeling the need to have something to say about each one in every category. This can also be a good format if you want to say that both subjects are appropriate in different contexts or for different people.

One-at-a-Time Model

    I. Introduction

        A. Hook

        B. Introduce subjects that are being compared

        C. Explain reason for comparing

        D. Give brief summary

   II. Body paragraph 1: Discussion of first subject

        A. Features

        B. Uses

        C. Good points

        D. Drawbacks

        E. Summary

  III. Body paragraph 2: Discussion of second subject

        A. Features

        B. Uses

C. Good points

D. Drawbacks

E. Summary

IV. Body paragraph 3: Conclusion

    A. Any information that didn't come up in the body

    B. Recommendation/preference of one subject over the other

    C. Reasons for recommendation, tying back to paragraphs 1 and 2

    D. Qualifications and caveats

Point-by-Point model

You can also organize your essay by key features of each subject. This allows you to do a more detailed, point-by point-comparison. It is important to choose features that apply to both subjects. These should also be features that are important to your reader. For example, imagine you are comparing two cellphones to help the reader know which one to buy. Readers might like to know how big and heavy the phones are, the cost, the quality of the camera, and which system they use. They are probably not interested in details about which company made them or how long it took to develop each phone. So these would make poor choices for features to outline in each paragraph.

You also want to make sure the features you choose tell something interesting. If you are comparing two tourist sites in your country, you will probably want to spend more time discussing the differences rather than the similarities. So if both are right next to each other, location would make a bad topic for a whole paragraph. Instead you can mention it briefly in the introduction or conclusion, You can also group several features into a larger topic. Perhaps you can have a paragraph about visiting that covers location, price, hours, and any kinds of restrictions.

I. Introduction

    A. Hook

    B. Introduce subjects that are being compared

    C. Explain reason for comparing

    D. Give brief summary

II. Body paragraph 1: First feature or topic

    A. Description of first subject regarding this feature

    B. Description of second subject regarding this feature

    C. Qualifications, caveats, additional information

D. Summary of comparisons

E. Recommendations

III. Body paragraph 2: Second feature or topic

    A. Description of first subject regarding this feature

    B. Description of second subject regarding this feature

    C. Qualifications, caveats, additional information

    D. Summary of comparisons

    E. Recommendations

IV. Body paragraph 3: Third feature or topic

    A. Description of first subject regarding this feature

    B. Description of second subject regarding this feature

    C. Qualifications, caveats, additional information

    D. Summary of comparisons

    E. Recommendations

V. Conclusion

    A. Any information that didn't come up in the body

    B. Recommendation/preference of one subject over the other

    C. Reasons for recommendation, tying back to paragraphs 1, 2, and 3

    D. Qualifications and caveats

Notice that you may not write everything exactly the way the outline shows. You may have 4 or 5 points to talk about. Your introduction may spill into two paragraphs. There may not be any qualifications or caveats. I hope, however, these outlines give you some kind of clear picture of how to organize an essay, and provide a structure you can adapt and change as needed.

Choosing good topics

It is always difficult to choose a topic for an essay. However, compare and contrast essays are particularly difficult because you can compare almost anything. Everything in the world has something in common and some differences with something else. You can even find similarities between a smartphone and a kitchen sink: both are used every day, both are a kind of tool, and both made people's lives much easier when they appeared. So how do you choose good subjects?

This book is full of general ideas, such as comparing two places or two cultural traditions. But it will still be up to you to decide exactly which subjects to compare. Because there are so many options, it's important to remember why you are comparing these subjects. Once you know your purpose, you will know who wants to read your essay. Once you know the reader, you will know what they are interested in reading about. That will guide to your topic. Or sometimes, the purpose leads you to the topic and then the reader.

As a general rule though, the two subjects should have interesting things in common and also interesting differences. That will ensure that comparing and contrasting have a purpose, that the reader will learn something helpful.

If you want to compare two books, think about why. Is it to explain why one book is better than the other? If so, you should choose two books that have features you like, but one is more successful or has more features. Or perhaps you want to show why a particular book is helpful for students of English. Then you might compare it to a book that seems helpful, but isn't, or a book that is focused more on passing exams than general English.

As we discussed, comparisons can also help you analyze a subject deeply. Sometimes to show why an event is important, it helps to compare it to another event that everyone agrees is important. Then you will want to choose two events that have interesting things in common. The differences between them should tell you something about the events.

Of course, as with any essay, you should write about things you care about. You should have something to say. And you should write about what you know, so you write accurately and with authority.

Useful Language for Persuasive Essays

To talk about similarities

similarly

and....too

also

likewise

in the same way

just as

in addition

both

as well as

To talk about differences

however

yet

on the other hand

by contrast

as opposed to

whereas

although

differ in

unlike

as opposed to

Other comparisons

as [adjective] as

[comparative form of adjective] than

less [adjective]than

To introduce an example

for example

such as

for instance

like

including

excluding

To give an opinion

I think that ...

It seems clear [to me] that

For these reasons …

Because of this, I believe that …

In short, …

Therefore

To make a recommendation

You might like …

People who … will prefer

I recommend… because ….

The best option is ….

X is better for people who….

There's no question, X is the best for …

If you're looking for something that is ….,
you should choose Y

COMPARE AND CONTRAST
Two universities or schools or kinds of educational institutions

↔

COMPARE AND CONTRAST
Two public attractions such as two museums or parks or historical sites

↔

_____
_____
_____
_____
_____
_____
_____
_____
_____
_____
_____
_____
_____
_____
_____
_____
_____
_____
_____
_____
_____
_____

COMPARE AND CONTRAST
Two stores or kinds of stores

←→

COMPARE AND CONTRAST

Two restaurants or kinds of restaurants, such as a family
restaurant, a fast food place, a café, or a pub

↔

_____
_____
_____
_____
_____
_____
_____
_____
_____
_____
_____
_____
_____
_____
_____
_____
_____
_____
_____
_____
_____
_____
_____
_____

COMPARE AND CONTRAST
Life in the city and life in the country

↔

COMPARE AND CONTRAST
Two places or kinds of places to go on vacation

↔

_____
_____
_____
_____
_____
_____
_____
_____
_____
_____
_____
_____
_____
_____
_____
_____
_____
_____
_____
_____
_____
_____
_____
_____

COMPARE AND CONTRAST
Two kinds of homes, such as a house or an apartment

↔

COMPARE AND CONTRAST
Two well-known natural features such as two mountains,
deserts, rivers, or beaches

↔

_____

_____

_____

_____

_____

_____

_____

_____

_____

_____

_____

_____

_____

_____

_____

_____

_____

_____

_____

_____

_____

_____

COMPARE AND CONTRAST

Two countries, thinking about history, geography, culture, the people, or other aspects

↔

COMPARE AND CONTRAST
Two regions of a country, such as two states

$\leftrightarrow$

_____

_____

_____

_____

_____

_____

_____

_____

_____

_____

_____

_____

_____

_____

_____

_____

_____

_____

_____

_____

_____

_____

_____

COMPARE AND CONTRAST
Two pieces of technology such as two kinds of phone or MP3 player or smart TV

↔

COMPARE AND CONTRAST
Your life now and your life in the past

←→

_____
_____
_____
_____
_____
_____
_____
_____
_____
_____
_____
_____
_____
_____
_____
_____
_____
_____
_____
_____
_____
_____
_____

COMPARE AND CONTRAST
Two different holidays

←→

COMPARE AND CONTRAST
Weddings traditions in two countries

←→

_____
_____
_____
_____
_____
_____
_____
_____
_____
_____
_____
_____
_____
_____
_____
_____
_____
_____
_____
_____
_____
_____
_____
_____

COMPARE AND CONTRAST
People's lives in your country in the past and now

↔

_____

_____

_____

_____

_____

_____

_____

_____

_____

_____

_____

_____

_____

_____

_____

_____

_____

_____

_____

_____

_____

_____

_____

_____

_____

_____

COMPARE AND CONTRAST
Two hobbies you enjoy or know well

↔

_____
_____
_____
_____
_____
_____
_____
_____
_____
_____
_____
_____
_____
_____
_____
_____
_____
_____
_____
_____
_____

COMPARE AND CONTRAST
How children are raised in two different countries

↔

COMPARE AND CONTRAST
Two popular dishes or two forms of the same dish

$\leftrightarrow$

_____
_____
_____
_____
_____
_____
_____
_____
_____
_____
_____
_____
_____
_____
_____
_____
_____
_____
_____
_____
_____
_____
_____
_____

COMPARE AND CONTRAST
Two sports or two sports teams

↔

_____

_____

_____

_____

_____

_____

_____

_____

_____

_____

_____

_____

_____

_____

_____

_____

_____

_____

_____

_____

_____

_____

COMPARE AND CONTRAST
A life spent living in one place and a lifestyle of traveling

↔

_____

_____

_____

_____

_____

_____

_____

_____

_____

_____

_____

_____

_____

_____

_____

_____

_____

_____

_____

_____

_____

COMPARE AND CONTRAST

Two different types of eating styles such as vegetarian, vegan, Paleo diet, gluten-free, or low carb diet.

↔

COMPARE AND CONTRAST
Two kinds of animals to keep as pets

↔

_____
_____
_____
_____
_____
_____
_____
_____
_____
_____
_____
_____
_____
_____
_____
_____
_____
_____
_____
_____
_____
_____
_____
_____

Name: _____   Date: _____

COMPARE AND CONTRAST
Two types of jobs

↔

_____

_____

_____

_____

_____

_____

_____

_____

_____

_____

_____

_____

_____

_____

_____

_____

_____

_____

_____

_____

_____

_____

_____

_____

COMPARE AND CONTRAST

Two ways to solve a personal problem you or someone you know has faced.

↔

_____

_____

_____

_____

_____

_____

_____

_____

_____

_____

_____

_____

_____

_____

_____

_____

_____

_____

_____

_____

_____

_____

COMPARE AND CONTRAST
Two people you know well

↔

COMPARE AND CONTRAST
Optimists and pessimists

↔

_____

_____

_____

_____

_____

_____

_____

_____

_____

_____

_____

_____

_____

_____

_____

_____

_____

_____

_____

_____

_____

_____

_____

_____

_____

COMPARE AND CONTRAST
Introverts and extroverts

↔

COMPARE AND CONTRAST
Two teachers at your school

↔

_____
_____
_____
_____
_____
_____
_____
_____
_____
_____
_____
_____
_____
_____
_____
_____
_____
_____
_____
_____
_____
_____
_____
_____

COMPARE AND CONTRAST

Two stereotypes such as sports-lover, hopeless romantic, alpha
personality, or a nurturer

↔

COMPARE AND CONTRAST
Two types of friend or companion

↔

_____
_____
_____
_____
_____
_____
_____
_____
_____
_____
_____
_____
_____
_____
_____
_____
_____
_____
_____
_____
_____
_____
_____
_____

COMPARE AND CONTRAST
Two types of roommate.

←→

COMPARE AND CONTRAST
Two types of parents or parenting styles

↔

_____

_____

_____

_____

_____

_____

_____

_____

_____

_____

_____

_____

_____

_____

_____

_____

_____

_____

_____

_____

_____

_____

_____

_____

_____

COMPARE AND CONTRAST

People who like to plan and people who are more spontaneous.

↔

COMPARE AND CONTRAST
Two well-known public figures such as two politicians or two actors, from history or current life

↔

_____

_____

_____

_____

_____

_____

_____

_____

_____

_____

_____

_____

_____

_____

_____

_____

_____

_____

_____

_____

_____

_____

COMPARE AND CONTRAST
People who like to wake up early and people who like to stay up late.

↔

COMPARE AND CONTRAST
Two ways to make friends

←→

_____

_____

_____

_____

_____

_____

_____

_____

_____

_____

_____

_____

_____

_____

_____

_____

_____

_____

_____

_____

_____

_____

_____

COMPARE AND CONTRAST
Two ways to lose friends

↔

COMPARE AND CONTRAST
Two kinds of music

↔

_____
_____
_____
_____
_____
_____
_____
_____
_____
_____
_____
_____
_____
_____
_____
_____
_____
_____
_____
_____
_____
_____
_____

COMPARE AND CONTRAST

Two stages in a genre of music such as early rock and roll and contemporary rock

↔

COMPARE AND CONTRAST
Two types of social media

↔

_____
_____
_____
_____
_____
_____
_____
_____
_____
_____
_____
_____
_____
_____
_____
_____
_____
_____
_____
_____
_____
_____
_____
_____

COMPARE AND CONTRAST
Two different pieces of art or kinds of art

↔

COMPARE AND CONTRAST
Two different movies or television shows

↔

_____

_____

_____

_____

_____

_____

_____

_____

_____

_____

_____

_____

_____

_____

_____

_____

_____

_____

_____

_____

_____

_____

_____

_____

COMPARE AND CONTRAST
Two different books or stories or book series

↔

COMPARE AND CONTRAST
A book and the movie adaptation of that book

↔

_____

_____

_____

_____

_____

_____

_____

_____

_____

_____

_____

_____

_____

_____

_____

_____

_____

_____

_____

_____

_____

_____

_____

_____

_____

_____

COMPARE AND CONTRAST
Fiction and nonfiction or prose and poetry

↔

COMPARE AND CONTRAST
Two characters from a movie, TV show, book, or play

↔

_____

_____

_____

_____

_____

_____

_____

_____

_____

_____

_____

_____

_____

_____

_____

_____

_____

_____

_____

_____

_____

COMPARE AND CONTRAST
Two ways to use creativity in your daily life

↔

_____

_____

_____

_____

_____

_____

_____

_____

_____

_____

_____

_____

_____

_____

_____

_____

_____

_____

COMPARE AND CONTRAST
Two streaming services or TV channels

←→

_____
_____
_____
_____
_____
_____
_____
_____
_____
_____
_____
_____
_____
_____
_____
_____
_____
_____
_____
_____
_____
_____
_____
_____
_____

COMPARE AND CONTRAST
High school and college/university

←→

COMPARE AND CONTRAST
Undergraduate study and graduate study

↔

_____
_____
_____
_____
_____
_____
_____
_____
_____
_____
_____
_____
_____
_____
_____
_____
_____
_____
_____
_____
_____
_____
_____

COMPARE AND CONTRAST

Two school subjects or two categories of subject such as the arts, the humanities, or the sciences.

↔

Name: _____   Date: _____

COMPARE AND CONTRAST
Two kinds of teachers or two kinds of students

↔

_____
_____
_____
_____
_____
_____
_____
_____
_____
_____
_____
_____
_____
_____
_____
_____
_____
_____
_____
_____
_____
_____
_____

COMPARE AND CONTRAST
A good teacher and a bad teacher or a good student and a bad student

↔

COMPARE AND CONTRAST
Two varieties of English

↔

_____
_____
_____
_____
_____
_____
_____
_____
_____
_____
_____
_____
_____
_____
_____
_____
_____
_____
_____
_____
_____
_____

COMPARE AND CONTRAST

Attending classes online or attending classes in person

←→

COMPARE AND CONTRAST
Studying a subject on your own and studying with a teacher

↔

_____
_____
_____
_____
_____
_____
_____
_____
_____
_____
_____
_____
_____
_____
_____
_____
_____
_____
_____
_____
_____
_____
_____

COMPARE AND CONTRAST

Different kinds of assessment, such as an exam, an essay, or a project

↔

COMPARE AND CONTRAST
Public school and private school

↔

_____
_____
_____
_____
_____
_____
_____
_____
_____
_____
_____
_____
_____
_____
_____
_____
_____
_____
_____
_____
_____
_____
_____
_____

COMPARE AND CONTRAST
Management and executive positions, or management and workers

↔

_____

_____

_____

_____

_____

_____

_____

_____

_____

_____

_____

_____

_____

_____

_____

_____

_____

_____

_____

_____

_____

_____

_____

_____

COMPARE AND CONTRAST
Two different materials and their useful properties

↔

_____

_____

_____

_____

_____

_____

_____

_____

_____

_____

_____

_____

_____

_____

_____

_____

_____

_____

_____

_____

_____

_____

_____

COMPARE AND CONTRAST
Two methods of organizing a project

$\leftrightarrow$

COMPARE AND CONTRAST
Jobs that pay a salary and jobs that pay an hourly wage

↔

_____
_____
_____
_____
_____
_____
_____
_____
_____
_____
_____
_____
_____
_____
_____
_____
_____
_____
_____
_____
_____
_____
_____
_____
_____

COMPARE AND CONTRAST
Two different departments in a company

↔

COMPARE AND CONTRAST
Two different companies

↔

_____
_____
_____
_____
_____
_____
_____
_____
_____
_____
_____
_____
_____
_____
_____
_____
_____
_____
_____
_____
_____
_____
_____
_____

COMPARE AND CONTRAST
Two different ways to organize a company

↔

COMPARE AND CONTRAST
A good supervisor and a bad supervisor

↔

_____

_____

_____

_____

_____

_____

_____

_____

_____

_____

_____

_____

_____

_____

_____

_____

_____

_____

_____

_____

_____

_____

COMPARE AND CONTRAST
Small companies and large corporations

↔

_____

_____

_____

_____

_____

_____

_____

_____

_____

_____

_____

_____

_____

_____

_____

_____

_____

_____

_____

_____

_____

_____

COMPARE AND CONTRAST

Goods and services, from a marketing, or economic, or business point of view

↔

_____

_____

_____

_____

_____

_____

_____

_____

_____

_____

_____

_____

_____

_____

_____

_____

_____

_____

_____

_____

_____

_____

COMPARE AND CONTRAST
Sales and marketing

↔

COMPARE AND CONTRAST
Management and executive positions, or management and workers

↔

_____

_____

_____

_____

_____

_____

_____

_____

_____

_____

_____

_____

_____

_____

_____

_____

_____

_____

_____

_____

_____

_____

_____

COMPARE AND CONTRAST
Two different materials and their useful properties

$\leftrightarrow$

COMPARE AND CONTRAST
Two methods of organizing a project

$\leftrightarrow$

_____
_____
_____
_____
_____
_____
_____
_____
_____
_____
_____
_____
_____
_____
_____
_____
_____
_____
_____
_____
_____
_____

Name: _____   Date: _____

COMPARE AND CONTRAST
Jobs that pay a salary and jobs that pay an hourly wage

↔

COMPARE AND CONTRAST
Two different departments in a company

$\leftrightarrow$

_____
_____
_____
_____
_____
_____
_____
_____
_____
_____
_____
_____
_____
_____
_____
_____
_____
_____
_____
_____
_____
_____
_____
_____

COMPARE AND CONTRAST

Two different companies, thinking about their philosophy, their
approach to business, structure, history, or something else

↔

COMPARE AND CONTRAST
Two different ways to organize a company

↔

_____

_____

_____

_____

_____

_____

_____

_____

_____

_____

_____

_____

_____

_____

_____

_____

_____

_____

_____

_____

_____

_____

COMPARE AND CONTRAST
A good supervisor and a bad supervisor

↔

COMPARE AND CONTRAST
Small companies and large corporations

↔

_____
_____
_____
_____
_____
_____
_____
_____
_____
_____
_____
_____
_____
_____
_____
_____
_____
_____
_____
_____
_____
_____
_____
_____
_____

COMPARE AND CONTRAST
Goods and services, from a marketing, economic, or business point of view

↔

COMPARE AND CONTRAST
Sales and marketing

↔

_____
_____
_____
_____
_____
_____
_____
_____
_____
_____
_____
_____
_____
_____
_____
_____
_____
_____
_____
_____
_____
_____

COMPARE AND CONTRAST
Friendship and love

↔

_____

_____

_____

_____

_____

_____

_____

_____

_____

_____

_____

_____

_____

_____

_____

_____

_____

_____

_____

_____

_____

_____

_____

COMPARE AND CONTRAST
Narcotics and alcohol

↔

_____
_____
_____
_____
_____
_____
_____
_____
_____
_____
_____
_____
_____
_____
_____
_____
_____
_____
_____
_____
_____
_____
_____
_____

COMPARE AND CONTRAST
Two religions or beliefs

↔

COMPARE AND CONTRAST
Two political theories such as communism and capitalism

↔

_____
_____
_____
_____
_____
_____
_____
_____
_____
_____
_____
_____
_____
_____
_____
_____
_____
_____
_____
_____
_____
_____

COMPARE AND CONTRAST
Immigrants, refugees, and colonists

$\leftrightarrow$

COMPARE AND CONTRAST

Two forms of government or two parts of a government, such as the legislature and the executive

↔

_____

_____

_____

_____

_____

_____

_____

_____

_____

_____

_____

_____

_____

_____

_____

_____

_____

_____

_____

_____

_____

_____

COMPARE AND CONTRAST
Two solutions to the problem of climate change

↔

_____
_____
_____
_____
_____
_____
_____
_____
_____
_____
_____
_____
_____
_____
_____
_____
_____
_____
_____
_____
_____
_____
_____
_____

COMPARE AND CONTRAST
Two ways to solve a major political crises in history or currently happening

↔

_____
_____
_____
_____
_____
_____
_____
_____
_____
_____
_____
_____
_____
_____
_____
_____
_____
_____
_____
_____
_____

COMPARE AND CONTRAST
The way senior citizens are treated in two countries

←→

_____

_____

_____

_____

_____

_____

_____

_____

_____

_____

_____

_____

_____

_____

_____

_____

_____

_____

_____

_____

_____

COMPARE AND CONTRAST
Knowledge learned from studying or reading books and knowledge that comes from experience

↔

_____

_____

_____

_____

_____

_____

_____

_____

_____

_____

_____

_____

_____

_____

_____

_____

_____

_____

_____

_____

_____

_____

COMPARE AND CONTRAST
Trusting first impressions or waiting to get to know a person well

↔

COMPARE AND CONTRAST
Two kinds of energy such as fossil fuels, solar power, wind power, or hydropower

↔

_____

_____

_____

_____

_____

_____

_____

_____

_____

_____

_____

_____

_____

_____

_____

_____

_____

_____

_____

_____

_____

COMPARE AND CONTRAST

Ways to settle a dispute or argument between two people or two countries

↔

_____

_____

_____

_____

_____

_____

_____

_____

_____

_____

_____

_____

_____

_____

_____

_____

_____

_____

_____

_____

_____

_____

_____

COMPARE AND CONTRAST
Two wars or battles from history

↔

_____
_____
_____
_____
_____
_____
_____
_____
_____
_____
_____
_____
_____
_____
_____
_____
_____
_____
_____
_____
_____
_____
_____
_____
_____
_____

Name: _____   Date: _____

COMPARE AND CONTRAST
Two ancient civilizations

↔

Name: _____   Date: _____

COMPARE AND CONTRAST
Life as a cat or life as a god

↔

_____

_____

_____

_____

_____

_____

_____

_____

_____

_____

_____

_____

_____

_____

_____

_____

_____

_____

_____

_____

_____

_____

_____

COMPARE AND CONTRAST

Two pop star personalities such as the innocent or the bad boy or the cute one

←→

Name: _____   Date: _____

COMPARE AND CONTRAST
Two unusual events, from history or your life or one of each

↔

_____

_____

_____

_____

_____

_____

_____

_____

_____

_____

_____

_____

_____

_____

_____

_____

_____

_____

_____

_____

_____

Name: _____   Date: _____

COMPARE AND CONTRAST
Hot fresh pizza and cold day-old pizza

←→

_____

_____

_____

_____

_____

_____

_____

_____

_____

_____

_____

_____

_____

_____

_____

_____

_____

_____

_____

_____

_____

_____

COMPARE AND CONTRAST

TikTok and Instagram, thinking about the kinds of people who
use each one, filters, features, and content

↔

_____

_____

_____

_____

_____

_____

_____

_____

_____

_____

_____

_____

_____

_____

_____

_____

_____

_____

_____

_____

_____

_____

_____

_____

COMPARE AND CONTRAST
Two superheroes thinking about power and who would win in a fight

↔

_____

_____

_____

_____

_____

_____

_____

_____

_____

_____

_____

_____

_____

_____

_____

_____

_____

_____

_____

_____

_____

COMPARE AND CONTRAST
A never-ending summer or a never-ending winter

↔

COMPARE AND CONTRAST
Living in a space station and living in Antarctica

↔

COMPARE AND CONTRAST

Parents who get deeply involved in their kids lives and parents who are detached

↔

COMPARE AND CONTRAST
American football and soccer

↔

COMPARE AND CONTRAST
Dinosaurs and dragons

↔

_____

_____

_____

_____

_____

_____

_____

_____

_____

_____

_____

_____

_____

_____

_____

_____

_____

_____

_____

_____

_____

_____

Name: _____   Date: _____

COMPARE AND CONTRAST
Two popular memes

↔

_____
_____
_____
_____
_____
_____
_____
_____
_____
_____
_____
_____
_____
_____
_____
_____
_____
_____
_____
_____
_____
_____
_____
_____

COMPARE AND CONTRAST
Two popular dances or dance moves

←→

_____

_____

_____

_____

_____

_____

_____

_____

_____

_____

_____

_____

_____

_____

_____

_____

_____

_____

_____

_____

_____

_____

Other Writing Journals from Alphabet Publishing

Reflections Weekly Writing Journal:
52 Prompts about You

Inspirations Weekly Writing Journal:
52 Prompts for Short Stories

Comparisons: 52 Writing Prompts for
Compare/Contrast Essays

Case Studies: 52 Writing Prompts for
Problem/Solution Essays

Agree or Disagree: 52 Writing Prompts for
Compare and Contrast Essays

We are a small, independent publishing company that specializes in creative resources for teachers in the area of English Language Arts and English as a Second or Other Language. We help stock the teacher toolkit with practical, useful, and innovative materials.

www.ingramcontent.com/pod-product-compliance
Lightning Source LLC
Chambersburg PA
CBHW081336120626
46546CB00011B/3372